WILD WORLD
ACTIVITY BOOK

GEMMA BARDER
AND
JENNY WREN

ARCTURUS

CONTENTS

ARCTURUS

This edition published in 2021 by Arcturus Publishing Limited
26/27 Bickels Yard, 151–153 Bermondsey Street,
London SE1 3HA

Author: Gemma Barder
Illustrator: Jenny Wren
Editor: Violet Peto
Designer: Jeni Child
Design Manager: Jessica Holliland
Managing Editor: Joe Harris

ISBN: 978-1-83940-725-3
CH007782NT
Supplier 42, Date 0921, Print run 11695

Printed in Singapore

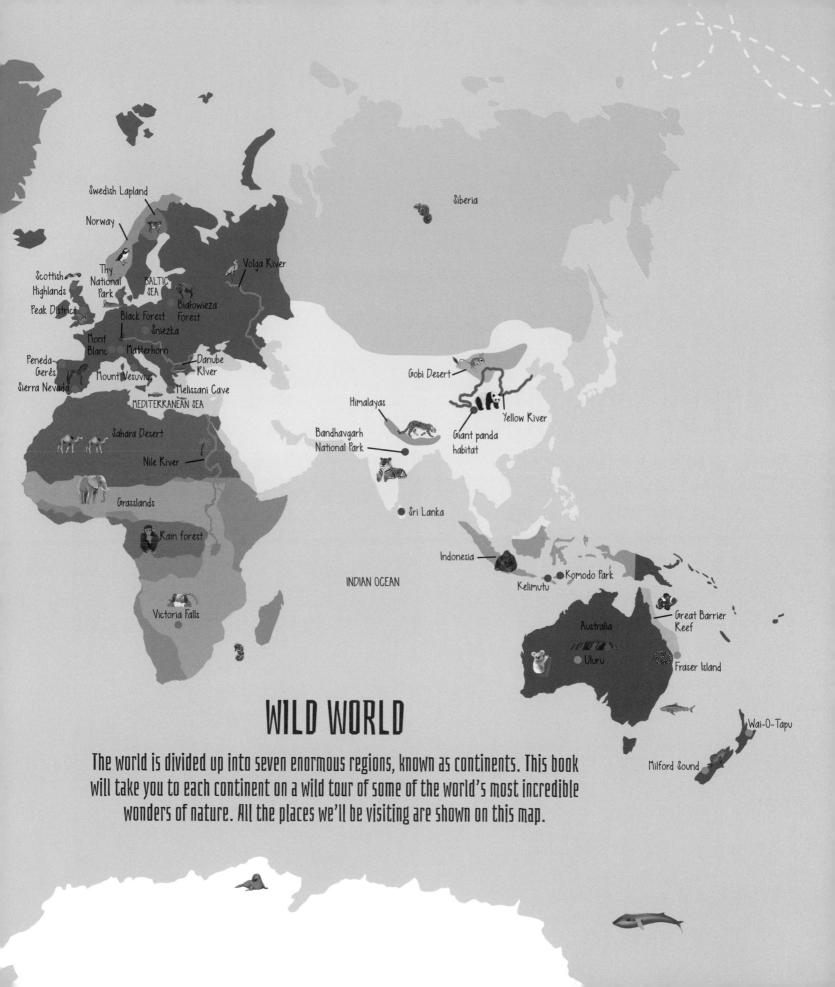

Swedish Lapland
Norway
Thy National Park
Scottish Highlands
Peak District
Black Forest
Mont Blanc
Peneda-Gerês
Sierra Nevada
Mount Vesuvius
BALTIC SEA
Białowieża Forest
Śnieżka
Matterhorn
Danube River
Melissani Cave
MEDITERRANEAN SEA
Volga River
Siberia
Sahara Desert
Nile River
Grasslands
Rain forest
Victoria Falls
Gobi Desert
Himalayas
Bandhavgarh National Park
Giant panda habitat
Yellow River
Sri Lanka
INDIAN OCEAN
Indonesia
Kelimutu
Komodo Park
Great Barrier Reef
Australia
Uluru
Fraser Island
Wai-O-Tapu
Milford Sound

WILD WORLD

The world is divided up into seven enormous regions, known as continents. This book will take you to each continent on a wild tour of some of the world's most incredible wonders of nature. All the places we'll be visiting are shown on this map.

ARCTIC OCEAN

Rocky Mountains

Athabasca Glacier

Yellowstone National Park

Lake Tahoe

Yosemite National Park

Grand Canyon

Mount Elbert

Mississippi River

Algonquin Park

ATLANTIC OCEAN

Everglades

Quintana Roo region

NORTH AMERICA

North America is the third-largest continent on Earth. From mountains to great plains, lakes, glaciers, and oceans, North America has it all! With so many exciting things to explore, North America is the perfect place to start our Wild World journey!

ROCKY MOUNTAINS

The Rocky Mountains (also called "The Rockies") is a large mountain range. It's so large that it covers part of Canada and the United States. As well as mountains, The Rockies also have the Columbia Icefield, which is a literal field of ice that feeds into six glaciers!

Mount Elbert in Colorado is the highest summit in The Rockies. Take a look at these pictures and see if you can spot five differences between them.

- Mount Elbert is 4,401 m (14,440 ft) high. That's about the same as 13 Eiffel Towers stacked on top of each other!

THE ATHABASCA GLACIER

The Athabasca Glacier in Alberta, Canada, is one of the most-visited glaciers in the world. The glacier's meltwaters travel a distance of 4,000 km (2,500 mi) to the north via rivers and eventually into the Arctic Ocean.

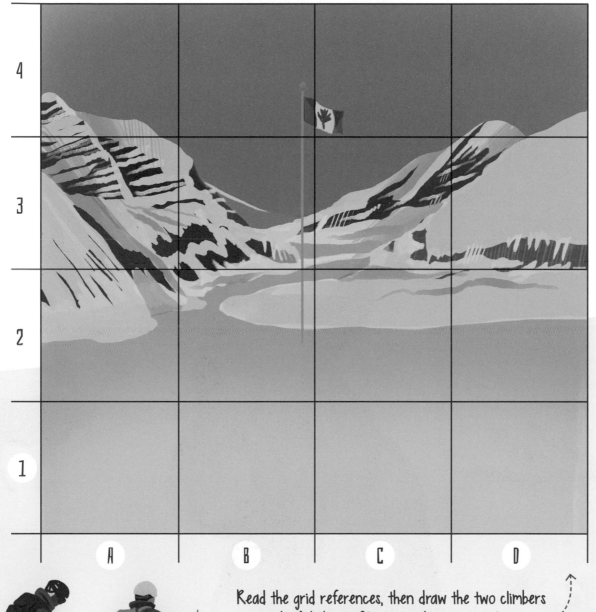

Climber one

Climber two

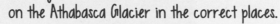

Read the grid references, then draw the two climbers on the Athabasca Glacier in the correct places.

1. Climber one is at A1.

2. Climber two is at D3.

- The Athabasca Glacier is shrinking due to global warming. Scientists believe it loses 5 m (16 ft) each year.

CANADIAN MOOSE

Moose are the largest of the deer family and can be found in various places all across Canada.

Give this moose some antlers, then read on to find out more about these amazing creatures.

- There are around 3,000 moose living in Algonquin National Park in Ontario.

- Moose love cold weather.

- Able to reach speeds of up to 56 kph (35 mph), moose are fast runners.

- Moose are great swimmers.

YELLOWSTONE NATIONAL PARK

Yellowstone National Park is really, really big. In fact, it's bigger than the US states of Rhode Island and Delaware put together! It has lakes, waterfalls, and geysers (hot water springs that shoot up into the air).

It's also home to grizzly bears, who get some of their food from rivers full of fish that flow through the park.

Use the space below to draw your own grizzly bear.

THE GRAND CANYON

The Grand Canyon in Arizona, USA, is one of the Seven Natural Wonders of the World. It is 446 km (277 mi) long and 29 km (18 mi) wide at its biggest point. It's a really important site for archaeologists and geologists, too, since the rock at the bottom of the canyon is thought to be millions, if not, billions of years old!

1   2   3   4   5

The bald eagle is often spotted swooping through the Grand Canyon, hunting for fish in the river. Can you complete this jigsaw puzzle? Which two pieces don't belong?

A   B   C

The Colorado River runs through the Grand Canyon. Before the Glen Canyon Dam was built, the river used to be a strange hue. Use the clue to figure out which one.

Clue: I'm used to make orange but not green. _____

EVERGLADES

The Everglades is a gigantic area of subtropical wetlands.
The water and grasses that grow in it are home to millions of plants and animals.

Visitors to the Everglades travel around in airboats, each powered by a huge propeller. Can you guide this boat through the 'glades? Watch out for alligators and crocodiles!

American crocodile

American alligator

START

- Both the American crocodile and the American alligator live side by side in the Everglades. It is the only place in the world where this happens!

Florida panther

- The critically endangered Florida panther lives in the Everglades. There are thought to be fewer than 100 left in the area.

- It is the largest mangrove ecosystem in the western hemisphere. Mangroves are small trees that grow in water.

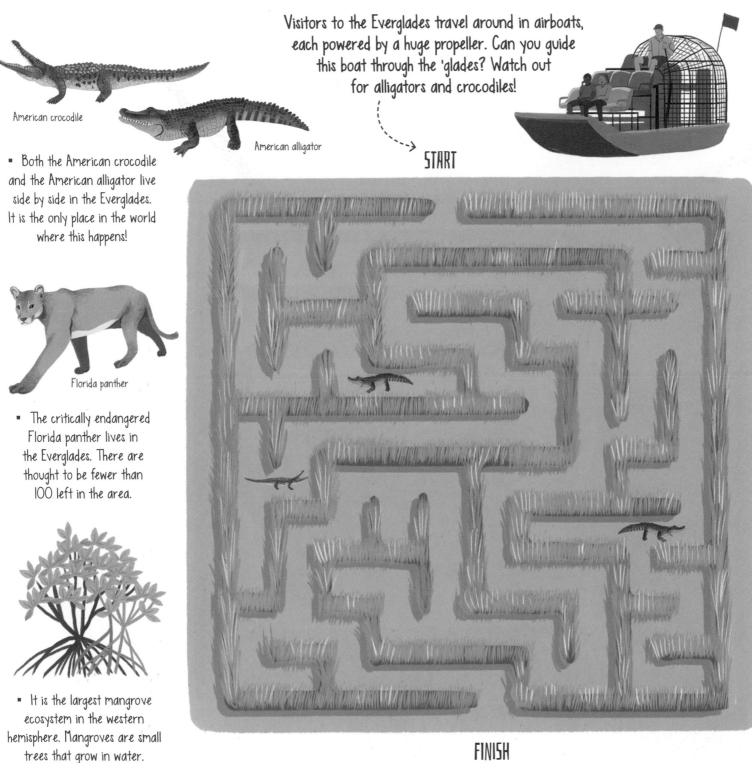

FINISH

ATLANTIC OCEAN

The Atlantic Ocean covers around 20% of the Earth's surface and touches the coasts of North America, Africa, and Europe. If you dive into the waters off the coast of Florida, you might just spot manatees, dolphins, and sea turtles!

Take a look at this image, and count how many of each animal you can spot.

Rock beauty   Dolphin   Sea turtle   Swordfish   Seahorse   Orca

THE MISSISSIPPI

The Mississippi is one of the most famous rivers in North America and flows through 10 states. The river is home to lots of creatures, including many species of rattlesnake, with some on the endangered list.

--- Can you match each snake to its exact pair?

A

D

C

B

G

E

F

H

I

J

K

L

The Mississippi is not a good place for swimming. The currents are very strong, and the water is said to smell and taste really bad!

LAKE TAHOE

Lake Tahoe is one of the deepest lakes in all of North America and certainly one of the most popular. As well as being surrounded by beautiful alpine forests, it's also home to lots of animals, including beavers, bears, coyotes, and even mountain lions!

Complete this sudoku by placing one of each animal in every row, column, and mini square.

Beaver

Coyote

Mountain lion

American black bear

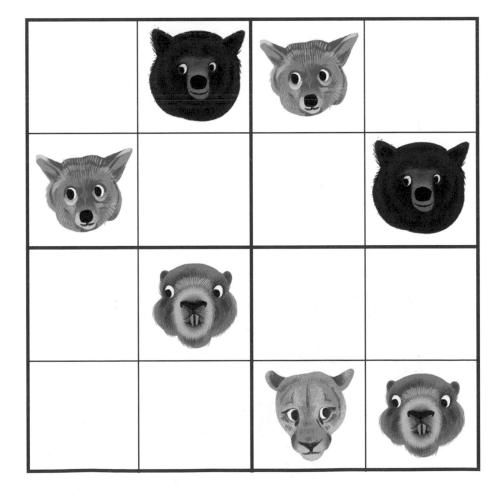

YOSEMITE NATIONAL PARK

Yosemite National Park in California is one of the oldest parks in the United States. It is famous for its giant sequoia trees and for having one of the world's tallest waterfalls.

Yosemite Falls is 739 m (2,425 ft) tall and is actually made up of three waterfalls running together. Finish this picture by drawing the waterfall onto the cliff edge.

Yosemite National Park is also home to the beautiful bobcat! These fabulous felines are a bit shy around humans, but they are very important to the park as they keep the rodent population down.
Can you find the matching pair of bobcats? Look closely at their stripes!

A
B
C
D
E

MEXICAN WILDLIFE

Mexico is so large that it has mountains, deserts, rain forests, and four different time zones!

In the rain forests of Quintana Roo live the Mexican spider monkeys. These long-limbed primates use their tails as well as their arms and legs to swing through the trees in search of food. Can you tell which lucky monkey has found the pile of figs (a food they really love)? _____

1

2

3

Wander through the deserts of Mexico, and you are sure to find lots of cacti—from tall and spiky to small and round like a ball.

Can you find three matching pairs of cacti?

A

B

C

D

E

F

THE ARCTIC

The North American Arctic is made up of the northern parts of Alaska, Canada, and Greenland. It is home to some incredible creatures that thrive in and around the icy Arctic Ocean.

Beluga whale   Caribou   Arctic wolf   Narwhal   Walrus   Adult polar bear

17

SOUTH AMERICA

South America is home to a huge variety of plant and animal species, making it the most biodiverse continent on the planet. From rain forests to mountains, deserts to oceans, South America truly has it all, and there is plenty to explore.

THE PACIFIC OCEAN

The Pacific Ocean is the largest ocean on Earth. In fact, it is bigger than all the continents put together! It stretches from the Americas all the way to Asia and Oceania.

Loggerhead sea turtles are found across the Pacific.

Can you match this turtle to its silhouette?

A

B

C

THE PACIFIC OCEAN

The Pacific is full of amazing creatures, from tiny krill to the gigantic blue whale. But climate change and pollution are affecting life under the sea.

Recycling our waste is one way we can keep it from ending up in the ocean. Take a look at this scene and count how many of each item you can find polluting the ocean.

7

THE AMAZON RAIN FOREST

Stretching over NINE different countries in South America, the Amazon is the largest and most important rain forest on the planet.

Thousands of species of animals call the rain forest their home.

- Despite being only 4 cm (1.5 in) long, the blue poison dart frog is extremely poisonous. It uses its bright markings as a way of warning predators away.

- Green iguanas can snap off their own tails if they think they are being carried off by a predator—and their tails will grow back again!

- Anacondas live in and out of the water. Although they are one of the largest and heaviest groups of snakes, they can move really quickly when swimming.

How many of each creature below can you spot in the main scene?

Golden tamarin

Green iguana

Anaconda

Blue poison dart frog

Sloth

The warm, wet weather in the rain forest makes it the perfect place for beautiful orchids to grow. Which two are exactly the same?

A

B

C

D

E

F

G

- There are thousands of different types of orchids in the rain forest, with new ones discovered all the time!

- Macaws can live for more than 20 years in the wild.

Use the number guide to finish the picture and give these macaws amazing plumage.

| 1 | 2 | 3 |
| 4 | 5 | 6 |

AMAZON RIVER

The Amazon River flows mostly through Peru and Brazil. It is the second-longest river in the world and is home to some amazing creatures, as well as humans! The Amazon River is one of the few places where you can spot a pink river dolphin.

Another pink species of animal that also enjoys the river is the flamingo!
Can you count how many there are here?

Use your pens and pencils to bring this river dolphin to life. Don't forget what shade they are!

Each year, naturalists travel along the Amazon River observing and researching the plants and animals that live there.

Can you make your way along the river, avoiding some of the dangerous native creatures along the way?

Piranha

Black caiman

Bullet ant

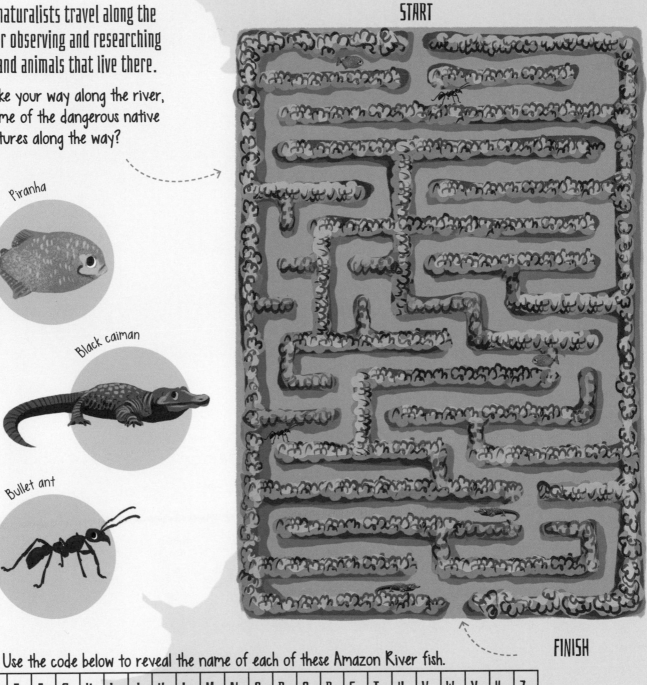

START

FINISH

Use the code below to reveal the name of each of these Amazon River fish.

A	B	C	D	E	F	G	H	I	J	K	L	M	N	O	P	Q	R	S	T	U	V	W	X	Y	Z
Z	Y	X	W	V	U	T	S	R	Q	P	O	N	M	L	K	J	I	H	G	F	E	D	C	B	A

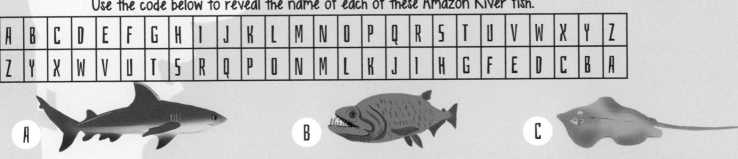

A   YFOO HSZIP

B   EZNKRIV URHS

C   KZMXZPV HGRMTIZB

_____   _____   _____

ATACAMA DESERT

The Atacama Desert in northern Chile is the driest hot desert on Earth. In fact, there are some areas where no rainfall has been recorded for hundreds of years! It is made up of sandy areas, rocky terrain, and salt lakes.

One animal that likes the dry surroundings is the Darwin's leaf-eared mouse. Complete this dot-to-dot to see what this little creature looks like. Then use your pens and pencils to finish the scene.

Mission to Mars

- Soil at the Atacama Desert is similar to samples taken from the surface of Mars.

- It has been used to test robots that are being sent to the red planet.

- The desert has been used as a filming location to look like Mars.

THE ANDES

The Andes is the longest above–water chain of mountains in the world and contains the highest mountains in both the Americas.

Aconcagua in Argentina is the tallest mountain in the Andes. In fact, it is the tallest mountain in the world outside the Asian continent. For that reason, it is very popular with climbers who want to take on a challenge.

See if you can figure out which of these climbers will reach the top of Aconcagua first!

A   B   C

- Aconcagua is 6,962 m (22,841 ft) tall. That's about the same as 50 times the height of the Great Pyramid of Giza in Egypt!

- It's actually an extinct volcano that was active 9.5 million years ago!

LLANOS

The Llanos grasslands stretch across Venezuela and Colombia. They have two main seasons —rainy and dry. During the rainy season, a lot of the grasslands are underwater, but it is also the time when wildlife and plants come to life!

The largest rodent in the world lives in the Llanos grasslands. Cross out any letter that appears four or more times to discover what it is called.

w c z a v z w z f w p z l y w d l d b f v f a r f d v v a l d l z

_____

The samán tree is one of the most recognizable trees in the Llanos. It looks like a giant umbrella and has clever leaves that fold when it rains. It also blooms with beautiful flowers. Copy the picture of the flower into the spaces on the tree.

ANGEL FALLS

Angel Falls in Venezuela is the highest waterfall on land in the world.
The water falls so far that it turns to mist before it reaches
the bottom. The falls are 979 m (3,212 ft) tall!

Use the grid to draw your own picture of Angel Falls square by square.

■ Thick forests surround the falls, which means
that it can only be spotted by air or on a boat.

■ Angel Falls is so big that it creates its own
weather! Add some weather to your picture.
Will it be sunny, raining, or cloudy?

■ When it is very rainy, the falls can split into two
separate waterfalls.

GALÁPAGOS ISLANDS

The Galápagos Islands are a group of islands in the Pacific. They contain some of the most fascinating animals on the planet, including iguanas, sea lions, penguins, and giant tortoises.

Marine iguana

Take a look at these Galápagos penguins. Can you match them into pairs?

A

B

C

D

E

F

G

H

Giant tortoise

- One of the most famous giant tortoises in the world was called Lonesome George. He was the last of the Pinta species of tortoise and lived to be more than 100 years old.

Sea lion

- Sally Lightfoot crabs play an important role in keeping the beaches of the Galápagos clean.

- They eat anything, from algae to food left behind by other animals!

A

B

C

- They were named after a Caribbean dancer, as they can effortlessly jump from rock to rock and run in any direction.

Complete the jigsaw. Which two pieces don't belong?

1   2   3   4   5

Galápagos racer snakes are found all over the Galápagos Islands, but the Fernandina species has learned to do something quite special. Can you guess what it is?

1. Whistle

2. Dig

3. Hunt underwater

EUROPE

Swedish Lapland
Norway
Scottish Highlands
Thy National Park
BALTIC SEA
Białowieża Forest
Peak District
Black Forest
Śnieżka
Mont Blanc
Matterhorn
Volga
Peneda-Gerês
Danube River
Sierra Nevada
Mount Vesuvius
Melissani Cave
MEDITERRANEAN SEA

Europe is the second-smallest continent on Earth and is in the northern hemisphere. It contains lush farmland, mountain ranges, and stunning coastlines. Find out more about some of the amazing places in Europe!

Europe is also home to around 6,000 different types of trees. Can you match these leaves to the trees they come from?

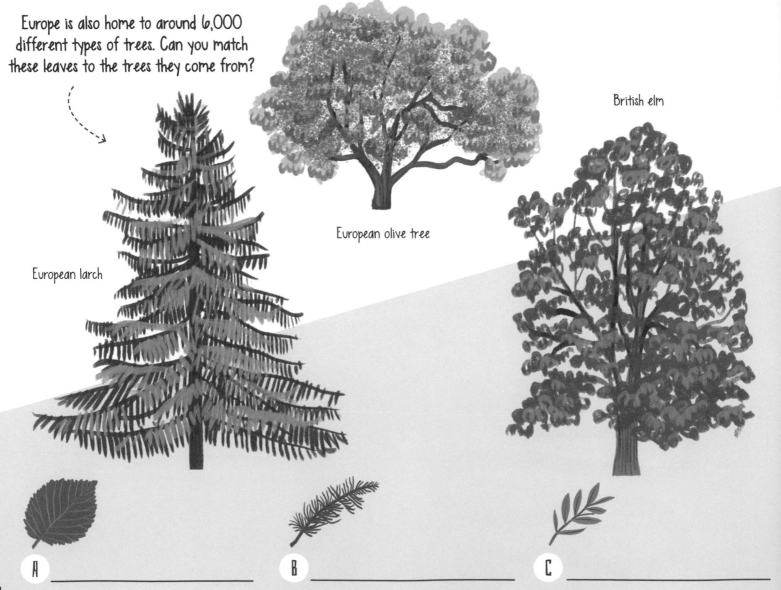

European larch

European olive tree

British elm

A _____

B _____

C _____

SCOTTISH HIGHLANDS

The Scottish Highlands cover the northwest of Scotland. With magnificent mountains, forests, and spectacular lochs (lakes), it's one of the most beautiful parts of the United Kingdom.

The Scottish Highlands is one of the few places in the UK where you can still spot a red squirrel in the wild, but they are very shy.

Can you count how many are hiding in the forest?

_____

Pine marten

Violets

Golden eagle

Wood anemones

Ben Nevis is the highest peak in the UK.

Can you complete this sudoku with some of the things you might spot on the mountain? Each one can appear once in every row, column, and mini square.

Ben Nevis

THE PEAK DISTRICT

The Peak District in Northern England was the country's first national park. It is home to rugged landscapes, caves, and farmland.

Fit the jigsaw pieces into the correct places. Which piece doesn't belong?

1   2   3   4   5   6

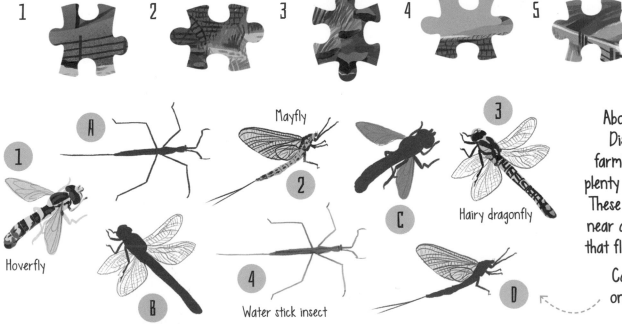

1 Hoverfly

A

B

Mayfly

2

4 Water stick insect

C

3

Hairy dragonfly

D

About 90% of the Peak District is covered by farmland, but there is also plenty of wildlife to be found. These insects can be spotted near any of the many rivers that flow through the district.

Can you match each one to its silhouette?

▪ The Peak District is also home to some incredible natural rock formations that were created more than 350 million years ago.

PENEDA-GERÊS NATIONAL PARK

Lusitanian salamander

The Peneda-Gerês National Park in Portugal is nearly 700 km² (270 mi²). It is full of mountains, green spaces, and forests. It's home to some incredible wildlife, including wild ponies, rare species of bats, salamanders, and some of Europe's only wolves.

Greater horseshoe bat

The Iberian wolf can be tricky to spot. Which of these matches the wolf perfectly?

Iberian wolf

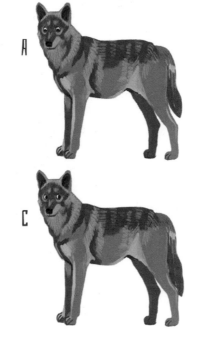

Follow these steps to draw your own Garrano pony.

- Wild Garrano ponies have been living in Peneda-Gerês for thousands of years. The breed was saved from extinction over 80 years ago but it is still one of the world's rarest breeds of pony.

Garrano pony

MELISSANI CAVE

The beautiful Melissani Cave on the Greek island of Kefalonia is a popular place to visit.
Inside the cave, there is a lake filled with crystal-clear water surrounded by trees.

Take a look at this picture of the cave. Can you complete the jigsaw? Which piece doesn't belong?

- Although it was known to the ancient Greeks, the cave and lake were only rediscovered in 1951.

- The only way to get to the cave is by boat along an underground tunnel.

THY NATIONAL PARK

Thy was the first place in Denmark to be called a national park. It has miles and miles of coastland, sand dunes, and pine trees.

Read these facts, and take a look at the picture, below. Turn the page to see what you can remember.

Common crane

- Cranes can be spotted off the coast.

Sea otters

Roe deer

Red deer

- Herds of red deer and roe deer live in the park.

- Cranberries and sea buckthorn berries are among some of the edible berries that grow in this area.

Sea buckthorn

Common seals

- Otters and seals can be seen diving in and out of the water.

Answer the questions below to see how much you remember about the Thy National Park!

1. How many seals were on the beach?

2. Were any of the cranes carrying fish?

3. What is the name of the plant in the picture?

4. As well as red deer, what other type of deer can be found in the park?

Red deer are the largest animals in the park.
They move in large herds across the landscape.

Which path should this red deer fawn take to return to its herd? _____

A   B   C   D

SWEDISH LAPLAND

Husky

Swedish Lapland covers a quarter of the country and is the only part of Sweden to border Finland and Norway. It is so large and wild that there are parts of Swedish Lapland where huskies outnumber people!

Lapland is also home to lots of other animals such as herds of reindeer, little birds called golden plovers, and families of lynx that like to hide out in the forests.

Reindeer

Golden plover

Lynx

Follow this sequence of animal footprints to find your way across the snow.

You can only move up, down, left, and right.

1 🐾

2 ⅄

3 🐾

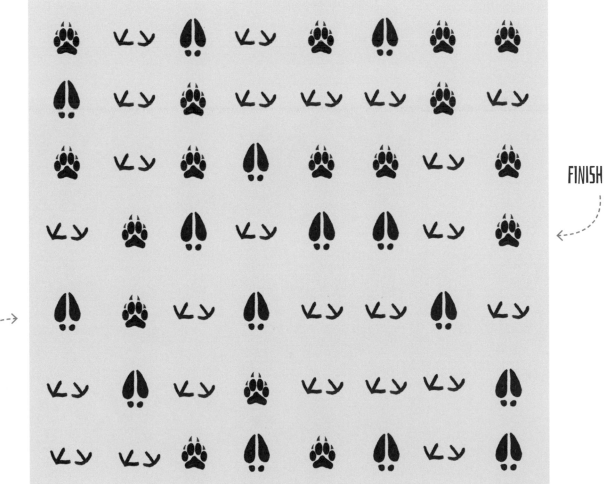

FINISH

START

NORWAY

Norway is part of a group of countries that make up Scandinavia. One of Norway's most beautiful features are its fjords (pronounced fee-yords). The fjords were created when giant glaciers disappeared, leaving clear waters surrounded by steep mountains.

Take a look at these pictures of a fjord, and see if you can spot five differences between them.

- The Sognefjord is the longest fjord in Norway and the third longest in the world. It is 203 km (126 mi) long!

- Around 300 species of birds make their home in Norway, including the puffin.

- Animals such as walrus, porpoises, and bearded seals can be spotted splashing in and out of the fjords.

- Water in the fjords rarely freezes, which means that it's the perfect home for lots of different types of fish, including coalfish and redfish.

BIAŁOWIEŻA FOREST

The Białowieża Forest is on the border of Poland and Belarus and is the last remaining section of a huge primeval woodland that used to stretch across Europe.

It is home to around 800 European bison, the heaviest wild mammal in all of Europe. European bison can grow to 3 m (10 ft) long and weigh 1,000 kg (2,200 lb).

Can you find the bison that exactly matches the one in this picture?

_____

A   B   C   D

These trees are commonly found in the Białowieża Forest. Read the facts and see if you can figure out which is which.

Small-leaved lime _____

Silver birch _____

Norway maple _____

Norway spruce _____

- The small-leaved lime has a broad trunk and an oval-shaped crown.

- The Norway spruce is a triangular-shaped conifer.

- The silver birch gets its name from the silvery-white tone of its bark.

A

B

C

D

- The Norway maple has a broad, rounded crown.

SIERRA NEVADA

The Sierra Nevada is a range of mountains in southern Spain.
It contains the highest peak in mainland Spain and is also home
to lots of native wildlife and plants.

The area is also well-known for its butterflies.
More than 120 different types of butterfly
have been spotted on the mountains.

Finish off this Nevada blue butterfly
by using the chart as a guide.

Despite the extreme
weather conditions
(hot, dry summers and
freezing winters) plenty
of beautiful plants
manage to bloom on
the mountains.

Crocus nudiflorus

Sky pilot

Sierra Nevada violet

1 2 3 4
5 6 8 9

THE BLACK FOREST

The Black Forest is a huge area
of evergreen forest in northwest Germany. It was
named by the Romans, who marched through the
tall, dark pine trees that cover the area.

Finish off the missing half of the picture
of this pine tree, then fill it in using
your darkest shade of green!

The Black Forest is the only place in the world
where a giant earthworm called *Lumbricus
badensis* lives. It can grows to 60 cm (24 in),
which is more than twice the length of an
average worm!

Can you figure out which of these
wiggly worms is the longest?

_____

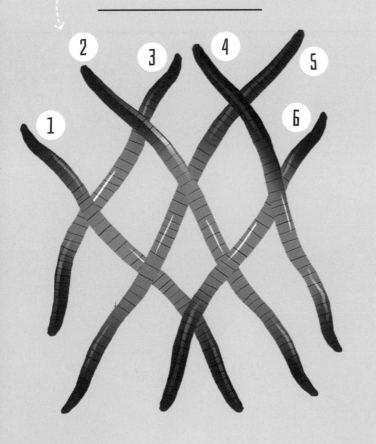

THE DANUBE

The Danube River flows though 10 countries and is the second-longest river in Europe. As well as being important for travel and drinking water, it is also home to millions of fish!

European eel _____

Huchen salmon _____

Sturgeon _____

Wels catfish _____

Zander _____

Burbot _____

Take a peek beneath the surface and see how many of each type of fish you can spot.

THE VOLGA

The Volga is Russia's national river and is the longest river in Europe.
Even though it is over 3,500 km (2,100 mi) long,
it starts and ends in just one country.

Can you decide whether these statements are true or false?

1. The word "Volga" means very long. _____

2. The river freezes for three months each year. _____

3. Some sections of the river are so wide that you can't see from one side to the other. _____

4. Russians call the river Father Volga. _____

One of the most common birds to living around the Volga river is the heron.

Can you spot five differences between these two herons?

44

EUROPEAN MOUNTAINS

Europe has some of the world's most famous mountains.

Take a look at these fact files, then cover the page and see if you can answer all the questions at the bottom.

NAME: Mount Vesuvius
COUNTRY: Italy
HEIGHT: 1,281 m (4,203 ft)
MOUNTAIN RANGE: Campanian volcanic arc
DID YOU KNOW? Vesuvius is a volcano. When it erupted in AD 79, it destroyed the Roman cities of Pompeii, Oplontis, Stabiae, and Herculaneum.

NAME: Matterhorn
COUNTRY: Border of Switzerland and Italy
HEIGHT: 4,478 m (14,692 ft)
MOUNTAIN RANGE: The Alps
DID YOU KNOW? The first woman to climb the Matterhorn was Lucy Walker in 1871.

NAME: Śnieżka
COUNTRY: Border of Czech Republic and Poland
HEIGHT: 1,602 m (5,256 ft)
MOUNTAIN RANGE: Krkonoše mountains
DID YOU KNOW? There is a chapel and a post office at the top of the mountain.

NAME: Mont Blanc
COUNTRY: Border of France and Italy
HEIGHT: 4,808 m (15,774 ft)
MOUNTAIN RANGE: The Alps
DID YOU KNOW? There is a tunnel underneath the mountain that connects France and Italy.

1. Which mountain is on the border of France and Italy?

_____

2. Which mountain has a post office at its top?

_____

3. Which mountain is also a volcano?

_____

4. Which mountain did Lucy Walker climb in 1871?

_____

MEDITERRANEAN SEA

The beautiful waters of the Mediterranean Sea are surrounded by 22 countries. Its name means "middle of the Earth," since that's what the ancient Romans believed it to be!

The sea is home to more than 700 different types of fish.

Can you complete the scene below, using these illustrations as a guide?

Small red scorpionfish

Zebra bream

Mediterranean parrotfish

Rainbow wrasse

BALTIC SEA

The Baltic Sea lies between Scandinavia and Eastern Europe. It is around 1,600 km (990 mi) long and can get very cold. In fact, it has been known to completely freeze over!

1

Lots of interesting mammals and sea creatures make their home in and around the Baltic, including this endangered porpoise.

Take a look at these pictures of porpoises and see if you can spot which two are exactly the same.

2

3

- The Baltic Sea was formed 10,000 years ago (which makes it the youngest sea on the planet).

- The sea contains both fresh water and seawater.

4

5

- The precious stone amber is found off the shores of Lithuania, Russia, and Poland.

South Shetland Islands   South Orkney Islands

ANTARCTICA

Antarctica is unlike any other continent on Earth. Its temperature is usually below freezing, and it is one of the driest and windiest places in the world. Although it is mostly covered in ice, it has a large mountain range (the Gamburtsev Mountains), a giant lake frozen under 4 km (2.4 mi) of ice, and a trench that could be bigger than the Grand Canyon. It's also home to some incredible wildlife.

SOUTHERN
OCEAN

Although there is no native population on Antarctica, thousands of people visit the continent for research and to spot animals.

Can you figure out where this penguin should be by looking at the grid references? Draw it in!

Start at 1A.

Go up 2 squares.

Go right 3 squares.

Go down one square.

5

4

3

2

1

A   B   C   D   E

PLANT LIFE

Most of the continent of Antarctica is covered in thick layers of snow and ice, but there are places where plants can grow, both in and out of the water!

A

B

C

D

E

- No trees grow in Antarctica, but two types of flowering plants can be found on the South Orkney Islands, the South Shetland Islands, and along the western Antarctic Peninsula.

One of these flowering plants is called the Antarctic pearlwort. It only grows to around 5 cm (1.9 in) and its tiny blooms are bright yellow. Count the blooms to figure out which of these patches of pearlwort has the most flowers.

- In the waters off Antarctica, there are more than 700 different types of algae! This tiny, often slimy, green plant might not seem important, but it plays a big role in Antarctica's ecosystem.

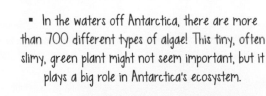

Blue whale

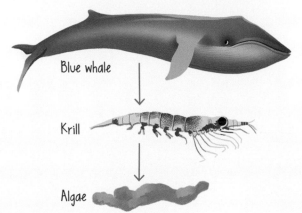

Krill

Algae

Algae is eaten by krill, which are then eaten by blue whales, seals, and penguins. Guide the krill through the maze, eating all the green algae on the way. Make sure you don't bump into any blue whales!

FINISH

START

SOUTHERN OCEAN

The Southern Ocean is the second-smallest ocean on Earth and certainly one of the coldest!
Water temperature ranges from −2 °C to 10 °C (28 °F to 50 °F)

Despite the chilly conditions, lots of animals call the ocean their home.
Can you match each animal to its perfect silhouette?

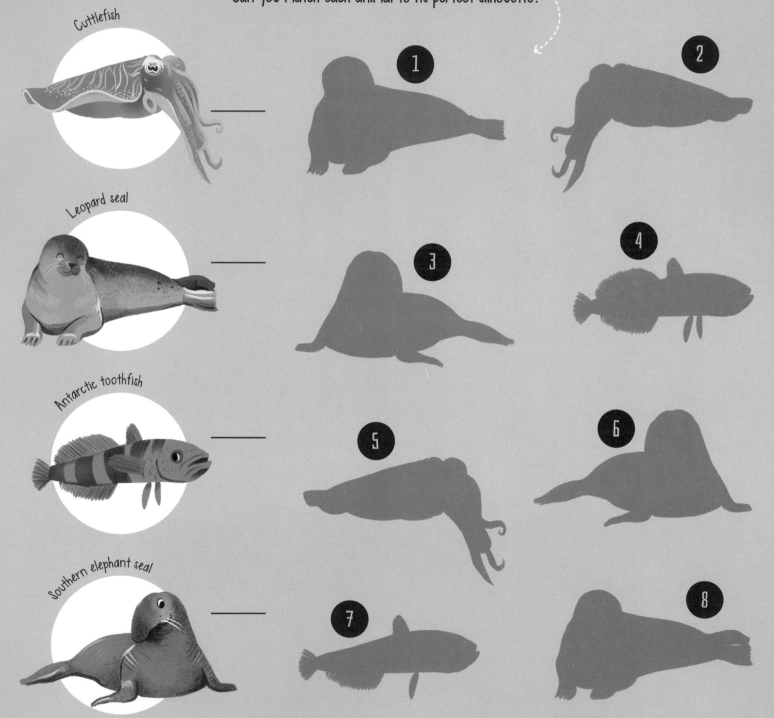

Cuttlefish _____

Leopard seal _____

Antarctic toothfish _____

Southern elephant seal _____

Two other incredible creatures that live in and around the Southern Ocean are the orca and the colossal squid.

- The orca (also called the killer whale) is the largest member of the dolphin family. It is very intelligent and can call to other members of its pod when it is time to go hunting!

Use this image to draw your own orca, square by square into the grid, then shade it in.

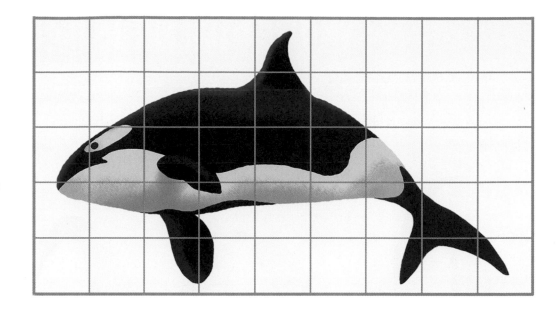

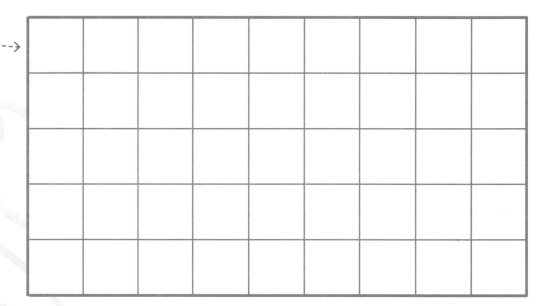

Colossal squid: True or false?

1) It can live for 40 years.

_____

2) It can grow up to 10 m (33 ft) long.

_____

3) Its giant fin is used for digging.

_____

4) It lives at depths of 1,000 m (3,280 ft).

_____

Fin

ANTARCTIC PENGUINS

The landscape in Antarctica is the perfect home for penguins. They have plenty of blubber (fat) and thick skin to keep them warm, and an ocean full of fish and krill to eat.

Take a look at these different types of penguin, then read the facts around the page to see if you can figure out which is which.

A _____   B _____   C _____   D _____

See if you can complete this sudoku. Only one of each penguin should appear in each column, row, and mini grid.

- Chinstrap penguins are named after the black feathers that wrap around the bottom of their heads.

- Just like other penguins, Adélie penguins live in large groups called rookeries for nesting. Adélie rookeries can grow to more than 500,000 birds!

- Emperor penguins are the tallest of all the penguins. They grow to an average height of 115 cm (45 in), which is about the same as a six-year-old human!

- King penguins are slightly smaller than Emperor penguins and look very similar. A king penguin has a solid orange patch on its cheek.

ANTARCTIC ANIMALS

Antarctica is full of amazing things to see.

Take a look at this scene, and count how many of each animal there is.

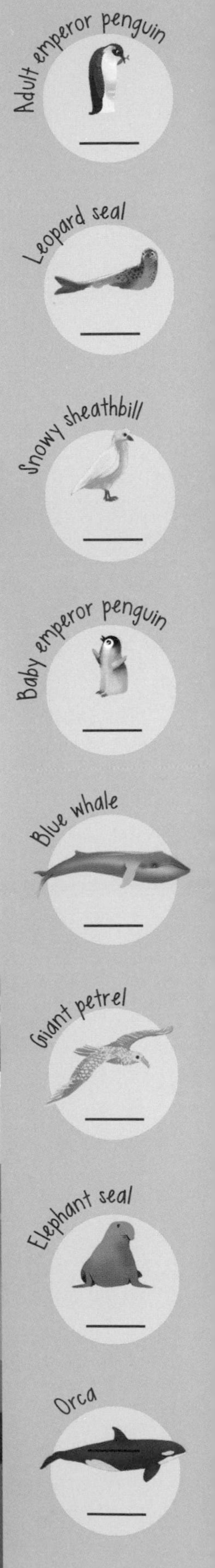

Adult emperor penguin
_____

Leopard seal
_____

Snowy sheathbill
_____

Baby emperor penguin
_____

Blue whale
_____

Giant petrel
_____

Elephant seal
_____

Orca
_____

RESEARCH STATIONS

Although there are no countries in the continent of Antarctica, lots of different countries support the area and conduct research there.

Take a look at these flags and see if you can draw a line matching them to their countries.

Then use the space to design the flag you would place if you reached the South Pole!

USA   France   Germany   UK   Italy   Russia   Japan   South Africa   Argentina

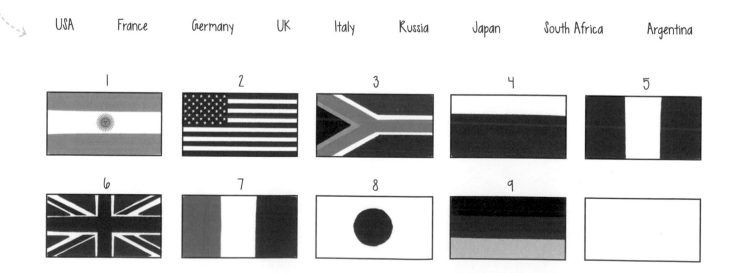

1   2   3   4   5

6   7   8   9

THE SOUTHERN LIGHTS

At the South Pole, a magical, natural light show can be seen across the sky.
These lights are called the aurora australis.

The light is made from tiny specks of plasma from the sun that react with nitrogen
and oxygen from Earth's atmosphere. The different hues created depend
on the type of gas that hits the plasma and the height at which they collide.

Finish this picture of the aurora australis.

MEDITERRANEAN
SEA

Sahara Desert

Nile
River

Grasslands

Rain forest

Victoria Falls

INDIAN OCEAN

AFRICA

The continent of Africa is the second—largest continent on the planet. It contains 54 countries and nine territories, and more than 1 billion people live there. In this section, we will learn about some of the amazing animals that live in Africa, as well as some very wet—and very dry—places!

- The Sahara is the largest hot desert in the world.

Africa is home to the longest river in the world, the Nile. It runs through lots of countries, starting in Lake Victoria and ending in the Mediterranean Sea.

Nile

Fill in the missing number in the sequence below to reveal how many countries it flows through.

5, 8, ___, 14, 17

Lake Victoria

- This spectacular waterfall boasts the world's largest sheet of falling water.

Victoria Falls

Table Mountain

- The city of Cape Town in South Africa lies at the foot of this flat-topped mountain.

ANIMALS IN THE GRASSLANDS

The African grasslands is a large area of tropical grassy plains. It spans across the middle and southern areas of the continent.

The grasslands are known for their wildlife, especially the amazing, large mammals that live there. Many tourists and conservationists spend hours tracking these animals for a glimpse.

Can you match these footprints with the animal they came from?

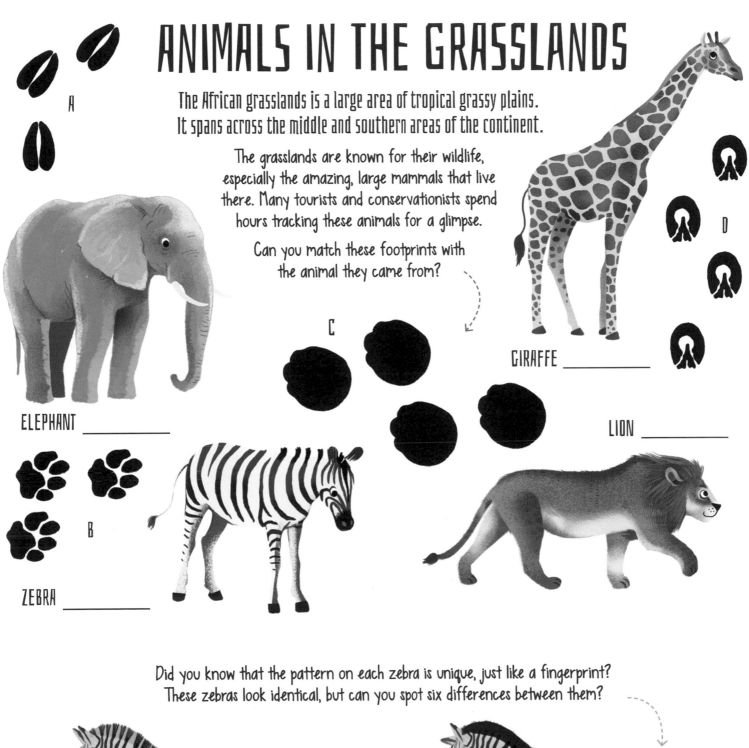

A

C

D

GIRAFFE _____

ELEPHANT _____

LION _____

B

ZEBRA _____

Did you know that the pattern on each zebra is unique, just like a fingerprint? These zebras look identical, but can you spot six differences between them?

ANIMALS IN THE GRASSLANDS

African elephants are the largest land mammals in the world. They can grow to over 7 m (24 ft) long and weigh up to 5,896 kg (13,000 lb)! That's about the same weight as three cars!

Take a look at this picture of an African elephant, then use the blank grid to see if you can draw it square by square.

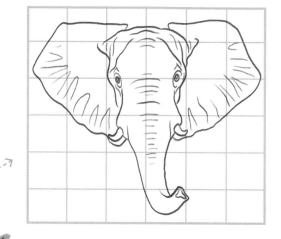 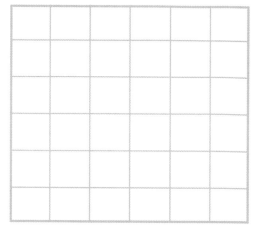

If elephants are the largest land mammal, then giraffes are certainly the tallest. Giraffes can grow to 5.5 m (18 ft) tall. That's about the same height as a double-decker bus!

Can you match these giraffe parents to their calves?

A

B

C

1

2

3

AFRICAN RAIN FORESTS

The Congolian rain forests stretch across the Democratic Republic of Congo. Together, they form the second-largest area of rain forest in the world.

This creature is called an okapi. It is native to the Congolian rain forests and lives mostly on fruit and plants.

Can you guess which animal is its closest relative?

1. Zebra

2. Giraffe

3. Deer

_____

Shade in each square using the coordinates to find out another amazing fact about these animals.

A3, B6, C2, D8, E7, F5, G2, H6

_____

	A	B	C	D	E	F	G	H
8	not	climb	the	bat	they	and	eat	not
7	The	babies	not	eat	poop	climb	and	climb
6	All	also	the	more	than	a	the	minerals
5	not	and	tall	human	snails	for	and	tall
4	climb	bite	aardvark	not	and	swim	not	size
3	They	and	climb	and	the	and	tall	buffalo
2	eat	can	eat	gorilla	tall	eat	extra	Tall
1	and	eat	not	biggest	not	climb	baby	climb

- Hippopotamuses are water-loving animals that live in and around the sub-Saharan lakes and rivers of Africa.

SAHARA DESERT

The huge Sahara Desert spans nearly a third of Africa
and is covered with giant sand dunes, salt flats,
and even mountains!

True or false?

1. The Sahara is the largest desert in the world. _____

2. It has snowed in the Sahara. _____

3. The Sahara changes size over the year. _____

The Saharan sand viper is a small snake of around 30 cm (11 in long). It hides from
its prey by wiggling its body under the sand, so that only its eyes can be seen.
How many sand vipers can you spot? _____

ANIMALS OF THE SAHARA

The dromedary camel is the perfect animal to live in the Sahara. It can survive on little water, and it has two sets of eyelashes to blink away any gusts of sand.

These camels are on their way to the top of the sand dune. Follow each path to see which one will reach all the way.

_____

A   B   C

This big bird also produces the biggest eggs. Can you complete the jigsaw? Which two pieces don't belong?

- The ostrich is the world's largest bird—it is also really, really fast! It can run at 70 kph (43 mph), which is nearly twice as fast as the fastest human can run!

1
2
3
4
5

A   B   C

AFRICAN PRIMATES

Africa is home to over 300 species of primates.

Take a look at these different primates, and see if you can match them to their silhouettes.

- Mandrills live in groups called troops that consist of an adult male, as well as up to around 20 females with their young.

A

Mandrill

Lemur

B

2

3

1

4

C

Eastern lowland gorilla

D

Bonobo

- The largest primate is the eastern lowland gorilla, which can weigh more than 200 kg (440 lb).

The African rain forest is the perfect home for great apes
such as gorillas and chimpanzees, who love to swing through the trees.

Can you help this baby chimp get back to its mother?
Using the KEY, swing through the forest, following the path one leaf at a time.

KEY   up   down   left   right

START

FINISH

THE INDIAN OCEAN

The Indian Ocean lies between Africa and Australia. It is the world's third-largest ocean and covers 14% of Earth's surface.

It surrounds over 1,200 islands including Madagascar and Mauritius, and is home to lots of different types of sea life.

Green sea turtle · Great white shark · Seahorse · Humpback whale

Take a look at these sequences to see if you can figure out which creature should come next.

A _____

B _____

C _____

VICTORIA FALLS

Victoria Falls is one of the most famous waterfalls in the world. It is part of the Zambezi River and is over 1,700 m (1 mi) wide and 108 m (354 ft) high.

When sunlight catches the mist from the falling water, great rainbows are formed. People travel from all around the world to see the Victoria Falls.

Take a look at these two images of the falls. Can you see five differences between them?

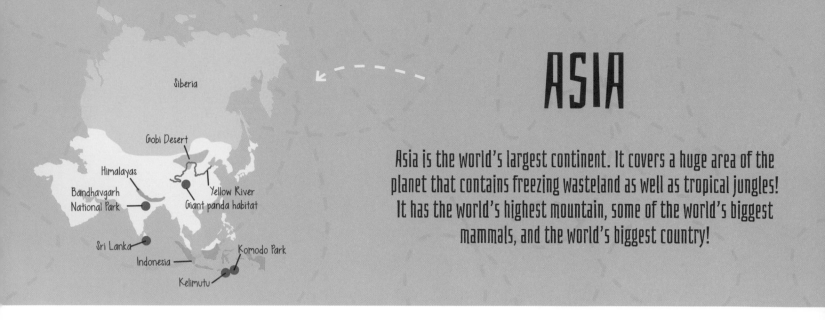

ASIA

Asia is the world's largest continent. It covers a huge area of the planet that contains freezing wasteland as well as tropical jungles! It has the world's highest mountain, some of the world's biggest mammals, and the world's biggest country!

Map labels: Siberia, Gobi Desert, Himalayas, Bandhavgarh National Park, Yellow River, Giant panda habitat, Sri Lanka, Indonesia, Kelimutu, Komodo Park

THE HIMALAYAS

The Himalayas are one of the world's most famous mountain ranges. They are found in South Asia and spread across several countries. They also include Mount Everest, the world's highest peak!

Hundreds of people try to climb Mount Everest each year. Take a look at this picture, and see how many climbers you can count.

ANIMALS OF THE HIMALAYAS

The Himalayas aren't just a row of snowy mountaintops. They have grasslands, pine forests, and scrublands where plenty of animals roam.

Snow leopard

Red panda

Himalayan brown bear

Himalayan marmot

Can you fit one of each of these animals into every row, column, and mini grid below?

KOMODO PARK

Komodo National Park is a collection of islands in Indonesia. It has been a protected site for many years because it is home to the komodo dragon, the world's largest lizard.

The komodo dragon can grow to 3 m (10 ft), with its tail as long as its body!

Take a look at the steps to draw your own version below.

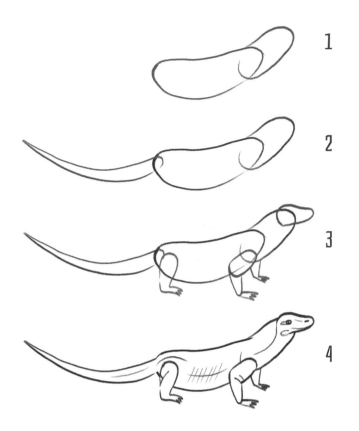

1

2

3

4

Adult komodo dragons don't have any natural predators. They prey on virtually any animal they can catch. Before baby komodo dragons can hunt, they have a very different diet.

Follow the instructions to find out whether they eat trees, grass, cicadas, or cattle.

Start at square A1.

Go up one square.

Go right two squares.

Go up one square.

Go left one square.

SIBERIA

Siberia is a large area of land in Russia known for its long, cold winters. It just over 1.3 million sq km (5,057,938 sq mi) and covers almost 9% of the world's surface.

Wolverine

Siberian chipmunk

Kamchatka brown bear

- Although it is very cold in Siberia (average temperatures reach -5 °C (23 °F), it isn't just a snowy wasteland. There are forests, lakes, mountains, and lots of wildlife!

Follow these trails through the snow to match each of these Siberian animals to their food.

Siberian rabbit

Pine seeds

Humpback salmon

TIGERS

Asia's most iconic animal is the tiger. There are six species of tiger left in the world, with numbers in the wild falling each year. They are: the Sumatran tiger, Amur tiger, Bengal tiger, Indochinese tiger, South China tiger, and Malayan tiger.

There are between 2,500 and 3,500 Bengal tigers left in the forests and wetlands of India, Bangladesh, Nepal, and Bhutan. Although this seems like a lot, they are classed as an endangered species.

The Bandhavgarh National Park in India is home to lots of Bengal tigers. Take a look at this scene, and see how many tigers you can spot hiding. See if you can spot some other animals that call the park home, too.

Bengal tiger

Bengal fox

Barking deer

Langur monkey

Common Indian krait

YELLOW RIVER

The Yellow River in China gets its name from the yellow silt and sediment that is picked up as the river flows. It's also sometimes called "the muddy river!"

Lots of birds, fish, and wildlife live in and around the river. Can you match these creatures to their correct silhouettes?

Red-crowned crane

2

A

1

Chinese pond turtle

C

Yellow River frog

3

B

D

- Due to global warming, parts of the river sometimes dry up completely.

- The Yellow River is important in Chinese history because it is seen as the birthplace of Chinese civilization. Many historical objects have been discovered along the river's edge.

E

F

H

G

4

Yellow River carp

GOBI DESERT

The Gobi Desert is the second-largest desert in Asia and covers parts of China and Mongolia. Unlike the Sahara in Africa, the Gobi Desert isn't very sandy. In fact, only 5% of the desert is covered in sand.

As well as being a famous place for discovering fossils, the Gobi Desert is home to lots of living creatures, too!

Golden eagle

Take a look at this scene for 30 seconds, then turn the page to see how many questions you can answer from memory.

Bactrian camels

Jerboa

Answer the questions below to see what you can remember!

 Jerboa

1. How many golden eagles were flying? _____

2. How many eagles were perched on a rock?_____

3. How many jerboas were there? _____

4. How many humps did each camel have? _____

5. Were any camels lying down? _____

 Golden eagle

Thousands of prehistoric fossils have been found in the Gobi Desert, from fossilized dinosaur eggs to one of the largest dinosaur footprints!

Can you figure out which fossil should come next in these sequences?

A

B

C

ASIAN PLANT LIFE

Flowers and plants in Asia are rich and varied. They are an important part of Asian culture and religion.

Read all about some of these famous blooms, then try spotting the five differences between these two pictures.

Orchid

In Asian culture, orchids symbolize love, beauty, and wealth. They are so popular that orchid festivals are held around the world each year.

Lotus

The lotus flower blooms on top of water. They are an important symbol of purity in Buddhism and Hinduism.

Frangipani

Although these flowers look pretty and have a sweet smell, they are seen as bad luck in some Asian cultures!

Cherry Blossom

Cherry blossom season in Japan is a beautiful and popular event. These tiny blossoms represent new beginnings.

THE GIANT PANDA

The giant panda lives in southwest China. It is one of the most-loved creatures in the world, thanks to its cuddly appearance. There are only around 1,800 pandas living in the wild, which makes them an endangered species.

Can you match these pandas into matching pairs?
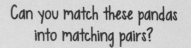

- Their black and white markings make great camouflage. The white parts are for the snow, and the black helps them to blend into the shade.

- Pandas love bamboo. It makes up 99% of their diet!

KELIMUTU

The Kelimutu Volcano is in a province of Indonesia. It is unique, thanks to three lakes that sit at the top of the volcano, each containing water in a different shade.

Depending on the time of year, the water in the lakes can be red, green, blue, and sometimes white!

Can you complete this jigsaw? Which two pieces don't belong?

!

2

3

4

5

A troop of long-tailed macaques live on and around the volcano summit. Draw them on these rocks by the volcano's edge.

INDONESIA

The country of Indonesia is made up of 17,508 islands,
but only 6,000 of them are lived on. The islands fall on either side of the equator.

It has thousands of miles of tropical wilderness, filled with wonderful animals such
as tigers, elephants, and orangutans, as well as some pretty amazing plants!

Can you figure out which is the correct
other half of this orangutan?

A

B

C

- The rafflesia plant is one of
Indonesia's national flowers and the
biggest flower in the world! But you
wouldn't want this giant bloom in
your house. It has evolved to smell
like rotting meat to attract flies!

Rafflesia

- The rafflesia plant
can grow to more than
1 m (3 ft) in diameter and
weigh 11 kg (24 lb).

SRI LANKA

Sri Lanka is a small island in the Indian Ocean off the coast of India.
It is the perfect home for plenty of wildlife, including tropical birds, giant mammals,
and more than 100 different types of snake!

As well as being home to the Asian elephant, Sri Lanka is known for its
endangered leopard population.

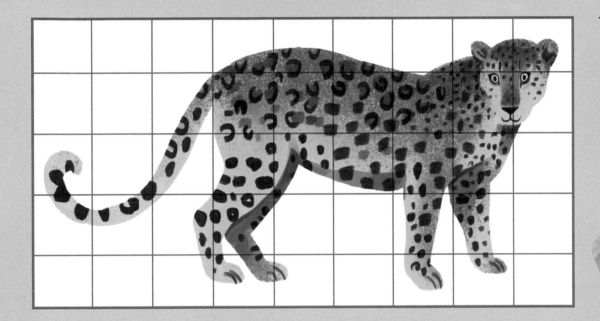

The Sri Lankan leopard lives in the jungles of Sri Lanka and preys on any other mammal it can catch! Since there are no tigers in Sri Lanka, they are the biggest cat on the island.

Draw your own leopard by copying the picture square by square.

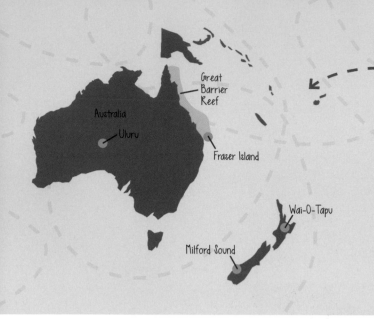

OCEANIA

Oceania is the smallest continent. It contains 14 countries and is mainly made up of ocean. There are more than 10,000 islands in the continent, too!

AUSTRALIA

Australia is the biggest country, and the biggest area of land, in Oceania. It is so big, it contains both snowy mountain areas and expanses of desert.

Australia is also home to lots of different types of marsupial—an animal that carries its young in a pouch.

Wombat

Koala

Can you match these facts to each marsupial?

1. It can jump up to 3 m (10 ft) in the air.
   _____

2. It lives in eucalyptus trees and eats leaves that are poisonous to other animals.
   _____

3. Its poop is cube shaped!
   _____

4. Its ears turn red when it is excited or upset.
   _____

Tasmanian devil

Kangaroo

SHARKS

The oceans surrounding Australia are full of amazing sea life. The most famous
(and sometimes feared) creature to live off the coast of Australia is the shark.
There are more than 450 types of shark on the planet, and 170 of them live around Australia.

Take a look at these different types of shark,
then see if you can match them to their silhouette.

NAME: Zebra shark

AVERAGE SIZE: 2.5 m (8 ft)

FEEDS ON: Snails, crustaceans, and small fish.

NAME: Whale shark

AVERAGE SIZE: 10 m (33 ft)

FEEDS ON: Shrimp, small fish, and plankton.

NAME: Tiger shark

AVERAGE SIZE: 5.5 m (18 ft)

FEEDS ON: Everything and anything!

NAME: Great white shark

AVERAGE SIZE: 5 m (16 ft)

FEEDS ON: Small sea mammals and fish.

A

B

C

D

ULURU

Uluru is a large sandstone rock. It has been a sacred ground for Australian Aborigine people for thousands of years.

- It is 348 m (1,142 ft) high, 9.4 km (5.84 mi) high, and covers 3.33 sq km (1.3 sq mi).

The distinctive thorny devil lizard is a common sight around Uluru. It can grow to 20 cm (7.8 in) and live for up to 20 years. Its diet consists mostly of ants. Can you see which of these spiky lizards will get to the anthill?

1

2

3

FRASER ISLAND

Fraser Island is the world's largest sand island (which means it is mostly made of sand). It is found off the coast of Queensland, Australia, and is also home to rain forests and mangrove forests.

These shells can be found along the beaches of Fraser Island. Can you put each one once into every row, column, and mini grid?

Carpet python

Red-bellied black snake

Marsh snake

Yellow-faced whip snake

Fraser Island is also home to plenty of snakes! Can you find three of each type of snake? Which snake is the odd one out?

THE GREAT BARRIER REEF

The Great Barrier Reef is a coral reef system that spans 900 islands off the northeast coast of Australia. It is so big, it can even be seen from space.

Living among the coral are some of the world's most bright and beautiful creatures.
Take a look at this scene, and see how many of each animal you can spot.

Angelfish

Clownfish

Starfish

Dolphin

Jellyfish

MILFORD SOUND

Milford Sound is a fjord on New Zealand's South Island. Its spectacular scenery includes mountains, waterfalls, and mysterious dark water that contains both fresh and salt water.

The water in the fjord is darker than most rivers and lakes. This is due to minerals that run off from the rocks surrounding the water. Can you match each of these animals to their swimming shapes in this picture?

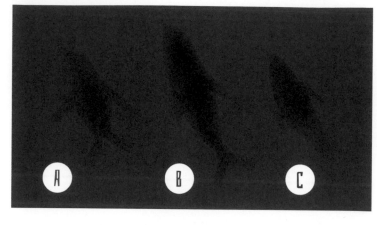

Milford seal

Little blue penguin

Hector's dolphin

Finish this picture of the Milford Sound waterfall.

WAI-O-TAPU

Wai-O-Tapu in New Zealand is known as an active geothermal area. This means that the landscape is full of boiling mud pits, naturally carbonated water, and geysers that shoot water high into the air.

Millions of visitors like to walk around Wai-O-Tapu each year and capture their memories by taking pictures.

Can you spot five differences between these two photos?

Can you guess what Wai-O-Tapu means?

1. Hot waters

2. Sacred waters

3. Strange waters

4. Angry waters

QUIZ

Now that you've been on a wild world tour, it's time to see how much you have learned! See how many of these questions you can answer. All the answers can be found on page 96.

North America

1. In which country is the Athabasca Glacier?

2. How many Florida panthers are left in the world?

South America

3. Are Amazon river dolphins blue or pink?

4. The longest above-water chain of mountains in the world is found in South America. What is it called?

Europe

5. What is the largest wild mammal in Europe?

6. What is the longest river in Europe?

Antarctica

7. Do trees grow in Antarctica?

8. Which species of penguin is the tallest?

Africa

9. On which river is Victoria Falls?

10. The world's largest bird lives in Africa. What is it called?

Asia

11. The world's highest peak is found in Asia. What is it called?

12. Which flower is seen as bad luck in some Asian cultures?

Oceania

13. How many islands can be found in Oceania?

14. What do thorny devil lizards mostly eat?

ANSWERS

PAGE 4:

PAGE 9:

PAGE 13:

PAGE 5:

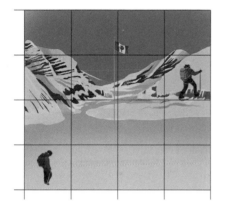

PAGES 10-11:

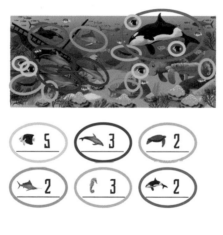

PAGE 14:

A and E

PAGE 15:

3

A and F

B and D

C and E

PAGE 8:

A4

B3

C1

Pieces 2 and 5 don't belong.

Red

PAGE 12:

A and E

B and F

C and H

D and L

G and I

PAGES 16–17:

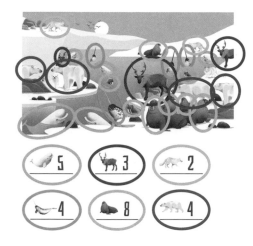

PAGE 18:

C

PAGE 19:

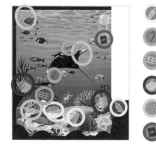

PAGE 20:

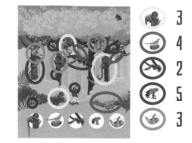

3
4
2
5
3

PAGE 21:

D and E

PAGE 22:

16

PAGE 23:

A. BULL SHARK

B. VAMPIRE FISH

C. PANCAKE STINGRAY

PAGE 24:

PAGE 25:

B

PAGE 26:

Capybara

PAGE 28:

A and G

B and H

C and F

D and E

PAGE 29:

A4

B1

C2

Pieces 3 and 5 don't belong.

3. They hunt underwater.

PAGE 30:

A. British elm

B. European larch

C. European olive tree

PAGE 31:

9 squirrels

PAGE 32:

A6

B5

C1

D2

E3

Piece 4 doesn't belong.

1C

2D

3B

4A

PAGE 33:

B

PAGE 34:

A3

B6

C4

D2

E1

Piece 5 doesn't belong.

PAGE 36:

1. Six seals were on the beach.

2. No cranes were carrying fish.

3. The plant in the picture is called sea buckthorn.

4. As well as red deer, roe deer can be found in the park.

C

PAGE 37:

PAGE 38:

PAGE 39:

D

1. B

2. D

3. A

4. C

PAGE 40:

PAGE 41:

5

PAGES 42–43:

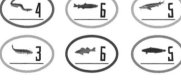

PAGE 44:

1. FALSE—it means wet.

2. TRUE

3. TRUE

4. FALSE—they call it
   Mother Volga.

PAGE 45:

1. Mont Blanc

2. Śnieżka

3. Mount Vesuvius

4. Matterhorn

PAGE 47:

1 and 4

PAGE 48:

D2

PAGE 49:

D

PAGE 50:

Cuttlefish—5

Leopard seal—8

Antarctic toothfish—4

Southern elephant seal—6

PAGE 51:

1. FALSE—it actually has a
   lifespan of only 2 years!

2. TRUE

3. FALSE—it is used
   for swimming.

4. TRUE

PAGE 52:

A. King penguin

B. Chinstrap penguin

C. Adélie penguin

D. Emperor penguin

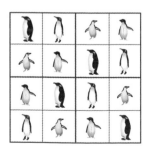

PAGE 53:

🐧	16
🐋	7
🐟	3
🦭	6
🐬	3
🕊	5
🐧	6
🦈	4

PAGE 54:

1. Argentina
2. USA
3. South Africa
4. Russia
5. France
6. UK
7. Italy
8. Japan
9. Germany

PAGE 56:

11

PAGE 57:

A. Giraffe

B. Lion

C. Elephant

D. Zebra

PAGE 58:

1B

2C

3A

PAGE 59:

2. Giraffe. In fact, the okapi is the only other living creature that is related to a giraffe.

They also eat bat poop for extra minerals.

PAGE 60:

1. FALSE—it is the largest hot desert; the largest deserts are in the Arctic and Antarctic

2. TRUE—snow has been recorded at the top of some of the mountains in the Sahara.

3. TRUE—the desert grows and shrinks depending on the season.

6 Saharan sand vipers

PAGE 61:

C

A3

B4

C5

Pieces 1 and 2 don't belong.

PAGE 62:

A4

B1

C3

D2

PAGE 63:

PAGE 64:

A.

B.

C.

PAGE 65:

PAGE 66:

30

PAGE 67:

PAGE 68:

5					
4					
3					
2					
1					
	A	B	C	D	E

Baby komodos eat cicadas.

PAGE 69:

Kamchatka bear eats humpback salmon.

Wolverine eats Siberian rabbit.

Siberian chipmunk eats pine seeds.

PAGES 70-71:

6

PAGE 72:

1G

2E

3H

4B

PAGE 74:

1. One eagle was flying.

2. Two eagles were perched on a rock.

3. There were two jerboas.

4. The camels had two humps.

5. Yes. Three camels were lying down.

A.

B.

C.

PAGE 75:

PAGE 76:

PAGE 77:

A5

B2

C4

Pieces 1 and 3 don't belong.

PAGE 78:

C

PAGE 80:

1. Kangaroo

2. Koala

3. Wombat

4. Tasmanian devil

PAGE 81:

A. Great white shark

B. Tiger shark

C. Whale shark

D. Zebra shark

PAGE 82:

3

PAGE 83:

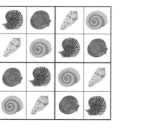

Odd one out: Marsh snake

PAGES 84-85:

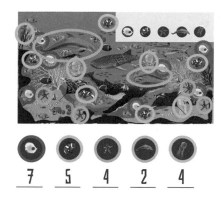

7   5   4   2   4

PAGE 86:

A. Milford seal

B. Hector's dolphin

C. Little blue penguin

PAGE 87:

2. Sacred Waters

PAGE 88:

1. Canada

2. Fewer than 100

3. Pink

4. The Andes

5. Bison

6. The Volga

7. No, but some plants do!

8. Emperor penguin

9. Zambezi River

10. Ostrich

11. Mount Everest

12. Frangipani

13. More than 10,000

14. Ants